# BOWL FOOD

## ONE BOWL RECIPES TO NOURISH YOUR BODY

Bounty Books

An Hachette UK Company
www.hachette.co.uk

First published in Great Britain in 2016 by Bounty Books,
a division of Octopus Publishing Group Ltd
Carmelite House, 50 Victoria Embankment, London EC4Y 0DZ
www.octopusbooks.co.uk

ISBN 978-0-7537-3122-2

A CIP catalogue record for this book is available from the
British Library

Printed and bound in China

10 9 8 7 6 5 4 3 2 1

Publisher: Lucy Pessell
Design Manager and Art Direction: Megan van Staden
Design: Wide Open Studio Ltd
Editor: Natalie Bradley
Project Editor: Jane Birch
Production Manager: Caroline Alberti

Cover photography, clockwise from top left: Front, Megan Van
Staden; Mirko Vitali/Dreamstime.com; William Shaw/Octopus
Publishing Group; Erica Schroeder/Dreamstime.com; Megan
Van Staden; Arinahabich08/Dreamstime.com; Arinahabich08/
Dreamstime.com; Catalina Zaharescu Tiensuu/Dreamstime.com;
Yulia Grigoryeva/Dreamstime.com; Jasmina976/Dreamstime.
com; Stephen Conroy/Octopus Publishing Group. Back, Marazem/
Dreamstime.com; Gkuna/Dreamstime.com; William Shaw/Octopus
Publishing Group; Luke Wilcox/Dreamstime.com; Stanislav
Valenga/Dreamstime.com; Annapustynnikova/Dreamstime.com;
Viktor Pravdica/Dreamstime.com; Sonyakamoz/Dreamstime.com;
Annapustynnikova/Dreamstime.com.

# CONTENTS

# INTRODUCTION

Bowl food perfectly reflects 21st-century attitudes to food. Increasingly multi-tasking, there's little time in our hectic lives for the array of plates and cutlery – plus the sink full of washing up – of a few decades ago. Instead, a bowl, a fork or a spoon and a relaxed attitude are what we want.

Stretched out solo on the sofa or sitting around the table with a group of friends, food in a bowl – from soups to salads and stir-fries to stews – is ideal for informal eating and the way we live now.

And it's so practical: a bowl in one hand leaves your other hand free to read a book, check your smartphone or feed your toddler.

## EATING LESS

Not only is eating from a bowl more relaxed, one of the key advantages of eating from a bowl is that portions tend to be smaller. Research has shown that using a bowl, rather than a large dinner plate, stops people from piling up the food and, if you don't over-serve, you don't over-eat. And using a smaller spoon or fork to eat your bowl of food can help too.

## MAKING HEALTHY CHOICES

Delicious though they undoubtedly are, the recipes in this book are also about nourishing, sustaining ingredients to promote health and wellbeing. Key to all-round nutrition are a few simple things:

**Eat seasonally** Enjoying fresh food in season means that you are eating food at its best, which is good for you, good for your wallet and good for the planet.

**Lots of fruit and veg** Basing your diet on nutrient-packed veggies and fruit is the way to health. Government guidelines are a minimum of five day (with the balance tipped more towards veg than fruit) but, for maximum health benefits, you should aim to get in seven portions a day.

**Go for good-for-you fat** Olive and coconut oil, oily fish and avocados are all sources of fatty acids for great skin, bones, nails and hair.

**Ditch the sugar** Sugar has been identified as being hugely harmful to your health so try to cut down on it. You should be aiming to consume a maximum of 30 g a day of added sugar.

## BEAUTY IN A BOWL

Eating out of a bowl doesn't mean you can't enjoy a special meal. Don't just sling it all in there – present your bowl of food beautifully so it's a feast for the eye. Choose an array of vegetables in vibrant colours and add a sprinkle for fresh herbs, a drizzle of natural yogurt or a wedge of lemon to garnish.

You can shop around for really pretty bowls, too, and have a variety of sizes and styles to suit what you're cooking – deep bowls for soups and stews to keep the heat in and wider, shallower bowls will be ideal for tagines, salads and so on.

# THE RIGHT BOWL AT THE RIGHT TIME

Try these recipe suggestions for the bowlful to suit your mood:

## NICELY SPICY

Spice up your day with these recipes, which pack a little heat.

## TV DINNER

Ultra-quick recipes if you're in a hurry to get out of the kitchen and catch up on your viewing.

## SUPER SLIM

Low-cal yet super-tasty recipes for when you want to watch your weight.

## LUNCH IN THE PARK

Light, fresh and transportable recipes to take out and about. Don't forget the bowls!

## WINTER WARMERS

Hearty, steaming bowls of comfort for when it's cold out there.

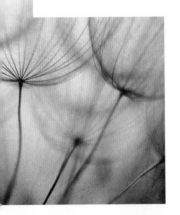

# ENERGIZING

WHETHER YOU WANT TO BEAT FATIGUE, EAT RIGHT FOR THE OPTIMUM WORKOUT OR ENSURE THAT YOU HAVE ENOUGH GET-UP-AND-GO FOR A DEMANDING DAY, YOU'LL FIND THE PERFECT RECIPE IN THIS CHAPTER.

# BROCCOLI & ALMOND SOUP

ALMONDS CONTAIN ENERGY-BOOSTING MAGNESIUM, WHICH IS ALSO ESSENTIAL FOR MUSCLE FUNCTION.

—

**SERVES 6**

**PREP TIME** 15 minutes

**COOKING TIME** 15 minutes

—

25 g (1 oz) butter

1 onion, roughly chopped

500 g (1 lb) broccoli, cut into florets, stems sliced

40 g (1½ oz) ground almonds

900 ml (1½ pints) vegetable or chicken stock

300 ml (½ pint) milk

salt and pepper

**TO GARNISH**

15 g (½ oz) butter

6 tablespoons natural yogurt

3 tablespoons flaked almonds

—

**1** Heat the butter in a saucepan, add the onion and fry gently for 5 minutes until just beginning to soften. Stir in the broccoli until coated in the butter then add the ground almonds, stock and a little salt and pepper.

**2** Bring to the boil then cover and simmer for 10 minutes until the broccoli is just tender and still bright green. Leave to cool slightly, then purée in batches in a blender or food processor until finely speckled with green.

**3** Pour the purée back into the saucepan and stir in the milk. Reheat then taste and adjust the seasoning if needed. Heat the 15 g (½ oz) butter in a frying pan, add the almonds and fry for a few minutes, stirring until golden. Ladle the soup into bowls, drizzle a spoonful of yogurt over each bowl, then sprinkle with almonds.

# MONKFISH & SWEET POTATO CURRY

SWEET POTATO CONTAINS IRON, POTASSIUM, MAGNESIUM AND VITAMIN C FOR INCREASED ENERGY LEVELS.

—

**SERVES 4**

**PREP TIME** 15 minutes

**COOKING TIME** 20 minutes

—

2 lemongrass stalks, roughly chopped

2 shallots, roughly chopped

1 large red chilli, deseeded

1 garlic clove

1.5 cm (¾ inch) piece of fresh root ginger, peeled and chopped

3 tablespoons groundnut oil

2 x 400 ml (14 fl oz) cans reduced-fat coconut milk

2 sweet potatoes, cut into 1.5cm (¾ inch) cubes

2 large monkfish tails, about 250 g (8 oz) each, cut into large chunks

2 tablespoons Thai fish sauce

1 teaspoon soft dark brown sugar

1½ tablespoons lime juice

2 tablespoons roughly chopped coriander, to garnish

**1** Put the lemongrass, shallots, chilli, garlic, ginger and oil in a food processor or blender and blend to a smooth paste.

**2** Heat a saucepan over a medium heat, add the paste and fry for 2 minutes until fragrant, then add the coconut milk. Bring to the boil and cook for 5 minutes until it reaches the consistency of cream. Add the sweet potatoes and cook until almost tender.

**3** Add the monkfish and simmer for a further 5 minutes or until the fish is firm and cooked through. Add the Thai fish sauce, sugar and lime juice, to taste. Sprinkle with the coriander and serve with some Thai sticky rice.

# RED MULLET WITH ORANGE COUSCOUS

THIS DELICIOUS RECIPES USES RED MULLET, WHICH IS A GREAT LOW-CALORIE, ENERGY-RICH FOOD AND PACKED WITH MINERALS.

—

—

**SERVES 4**

**PREP TIME** 15 minutes

**COOKING TIME** 15 minutes

—

4 red mullet fillets, about 150 g (5 oz) each

4 tablespoons olive oil, plus extra for oiling

finely grated rind and juice of 1 orange, plus 1 whole orange

4 sprigs of thyme

375 g (12 oz) couscous

400 ml (14 fl oz) hot vegetable stock (see page 125 for homemade)

finely grated rind and juice of ½ lemon

100 g (3½ oz) radishes, thinly sliced

75 g (3 oz) pitted black olives, chopped

handful of flat leaf parsley, chopped

salt and pepper

**1** Place the fish fillets on a lightly oiled baking sheet. Season well, then drizzle over 1 tablespoon of the oil and a little of the orange juice and scatter with the thyme sprigs. Place in a preheated oven, 180˚C (350˚F), Gas Mark 4, for 15 minutes until just cooked through.

**2** Meanwhile, place the couscous in a large bowl. Pour over the hot stock, cover and leave for 5–10 minutes until all the liquid is absorbed and the couscous has swelled. Add the orange and lemon rind with a little more of the orange juice, the lemon juice and the remaining oil, then leave to cool.

**3** Peel the remaining orange, discarding any white pith, then cut into small pieces and stir through with a fork, breaking up any clumps. Season and add the radishes, olives and parsley just before serving with the fish.

# JAPANESE TUNA SOBA NOODLES

SOBA NOODLES ARE MADE FROM BUCKWHEAT FLOUR, SO ARE AN EXCELLENT GLUTEN-FREE CHOICE.

**SERVES 2**

**PREP TIME** 10 minutes

**COOKING TIME** 10 minutes

—

200 g (7 oz) dried soba noodles

1 tablespoon vegetable oil

2 tuna steaks, about 125 g (4 oz) each

¼ cucumber, sliced

2 spring onions, sliced

2 tablespoons soy sauce

2 tablespoons mirin

juice of ½ lime

2 teaspoons caster sugar

salt and pepper

sesame seeds, to serve

**1** Cook the noodles according to the pack instructions. Meanwhile, heat a griddle pan until smoking hot. Rub the oil over the tuna steaks and season well. Cook on the pan for 1–2 minutes on each side or until charred on the outside but still rare inside.

**2** Drain the noodles, cool under cold running water and drain again, then divide between bowls.

**3** Cut the tuna into slices and toss together with the cucumber and spring onions. Mix together the soy sauce, mirin, lime juice and sugar until the sugar has dissolved. Pour over the noodles and sprinkle with sesame seeds to serve.

# TURKEY CHILLI POBLANO

THIS SPICY MEXICAN DISH INCLUDES A HINT OF DARK CHOCOLATE, WHICH COMBINES WITH THE LEAN PROTEIN IN TURKEY FOR A DOUBLE DOSE OF ENERGY-BOOSTING INGREDIENTS.

—

**SERVES 6**

**PREP TIME** 25 minutes

**COOKING TIME** 1 hour

—

125 g (4 oz) flaked almonds

50 g (2 oz) peanuts

½ tablespoon coriander seeds

1 teaspoon ground cloves

3 tablespoons sesame seeds

½ cinnamon stick

1 teaspoon fennel seeds or aniseed

4 large dried chillies

1 green jalapeño chilli, chopped

400 g (13 oz) can chopped tomatoes

75 g (3 oz) raisins

6 tablespoons vegetable oil

2 onions, finely chopped

3 garlic cloves, crushed

625 g (1¼ lb) turkey fillets, finely sliced or cubed

300 ml (½ pint) vegetable stock (see page 125 for homemade)

50 g (2 oz) bitter plain chocolate, roughly chopped

red and green chillies, finely chopped, to garnish

—

**1** Spread the almonds, peanuts, coriander seeds, cloves, sesame seeds, cinnamon, fennel or aniseed and dried chillies over a baking sheet and roast in a preheated oven, 200°C (400°F), Gas Mark 6, for 10 minutes, stirring once or twice.

**2** Remove from the oven and put the nuts and spices in a food processor or blender and process until well combined. Add the chopped green chilli and process once more until well mixed.

**3** Spoon the spice mixture into a bowl and mix in the tomatoes and raisins.

**4** Heat the oil in a large saucepan and fry the onions and garlic with the turkey on all sides until browned. Remove the turkey and set aside.

**5** Add the spice mixture to the oil remaining in the saucepan and cook, stirring frequently, for 5–6 minutes or until the spice paste has heated through and is bubbling. Add the stock and chocolate and simmer gently until the chocolate has melted.

**6** Reduce the heat, return the turkey to the pan and mix well. Cover the pan and simmer gently for 30 minutes, adding extra water if the sauce begins to dry out. Garnish with the chopped red and green chillies.

# CITRUS CHICKEN WITH RICE SALAD

THE HIGH LEVELS OF VITAMIN C IN CITRUS FRUIT INCREASE THE AMOUNT OF OXYGEN CIRCULATING IN THE BRAIN TO REFRESH AND GIVE YOU AN ENERGY BOOST.

—

—

**SERVES 2**

**PREP TIME** 10 minutes,
  plus marinating

**COOKING TIME** 15 minutes

—

2 boneless, skinless chicken
  breasts, sliced lengthways
  into strips

2 tablespoons buttermilk

grated rind and juice of
  ½ lime

1 garlic clove, crushed

**RICE SALAD**

100 g (3½ oz) mixed
  basmati and wild rice

1 tablespoon olive oil

4 spring onions, sliced

25 g (1 oz) cashew nuts,
  roughly chopped

handful of baby leaf spinach

grated rind and juice of
  1 orange

1 tablespoon soy sauce

**1** Put the chicken strips in a non-metallic dish. Mix together the buttermilk, lime rind and juice and garlic, pour the mixture over the chicken, turn to coat evenly and set aside for at least 10 minutes. Alternatively, prepare the marinade in the morning and leave the chicken in it in the refrigerator all day.

**2** Cook the rice according to the instructions on the packet. Drain thoroughly.

**3** Heat the oil in a small frying pan. Fry the spring onions for 1 minute. Toss the spring onions through the rice, and then add the cashew nuts, spinach, orange rind and juice and soy sauce. Set aside.

**4** Thread the chicken evenly on 4 skewers and cook, turning from time to time, under a preheated hot grill for 4–5 minutes. Serve with the rice salad.

# BRAISED LENTILS WITH GREMOLATA

A PERFECT COMBINATION OF SLOWLY DIGESTED PROTEIN, COMPLEX CARBOHYDRATES AND FIBRE, LENTILS ARE THE IDEAL ENERGY FOOD.

—

—

**SERVES 4**

**PREP TIME** 5 minutes

**COOKING TIME** 25 minutes

—

50 g (2 oz) butter

1 onion, chopped

2 celery sticks, sliced

2 carrots, sliced

175 g (6 oz) Puy lentils, rinsed

600 ml (1 pint) vegetable stock (see page 125 for homemade)

250 ml (8 fl oz) dry white wine

2 bay leaves

2 tablespoons chopped thyme

3 tablespoons olive oil

325 g (11 oz) mushrooms, sliced

salt and pepper

GREMOLATA

2 tablespoons chopped parsley

finely grated rind of 1 lemon

2 garlic cloves, chopped

**1** Melt the butter in a saucepan and fry the onion, celery and carrots for 3 minutes. Add the Puy lentils, stock, wine, herbs and a little salt and pepper. Bring to the boil, then reduce the heat and simmer gently, uncovered, for about 20 minutes or until the lentils are tender.

**2** Meanwhile, mix together the ingredients for the gremolata.

**3** Heat the oil in a frying pan. Add the mushrooms and fry for about 2 minutes until golden. Season lightly with salt and pepper.

**4** Ladle the lentils on to plates, top with the mushrooms and serve scattered with the gremolata.

# CHILLI & SPROUTING BROCCOLI PASTA WITH POACHED EGGS

THE IDEAL DISH FOR A HECTIC DAY, THIS HAS PROTEIN IN EGGS TO KEEP YOU GOING FOR A LONG PERIOD, PLUS CHROMIUM-RICH BROCCOLI FOR AN ADDITIONAL BOOST.

—

**SERVES 4**

**PREP TIME** 5 minutes

**COOKING TIME** 15 minutes

—

300 g (10 oz) linguine

250 g (8 oz) purple sprouting broccoli

4 eggs

2 tablespoons olive oil

6 spring onions, sliced

1 teaspoon dried chilli flakes

12 cherry tomatoes, halved

—

**1** Cook the pasta in a large saucepan of boiling water for 6 minutes. Add the broccoli and cook for a further 4–5 minutes until the pasta is al dente and the broccoli is tender.

**2** Meanwhile, bring a saucepan of water to a gentle simmer and stir with a large spoon to create a swirl. Break 2 of the eggs into the water and cook for 3 minutes. Remove with a slotted spoon and keep warm. Repeat with the remaining eggs.

**3** Drain the pasta and broccoli and keep warm. Heat the oil in the pasta pan, add the spring onions, chilli flakes and tomatoes and fry, stirring, for 2–3 minutes. Return the pasta and broccoli to the pan and toss well to coat with the chilli oil.

**4** Serve the pasta topped with the poached eggs.

# ZINGY WILD MUSHROOM RICE

A LARGE HANDFUL OF MUSHROOMS PROVIDES NEARLY 50 PER CENT OF YOUR DAILY SERVING OF IRON, WHICH IS KEY TO BEATING FATIGUE.

—

**SERVES 4**

**PREP TIME** 5 minutes

**COOKING TIME** 30 minutes

—

25 g (1 oz) butter

1 tablespoon olive oil

200 g (7 oz) wild mushrooms, trimmed and roughly chopped

1 onion, finely chopped

2 garlic cloves, crushed

250 g (8 oz) mixed wild and basmati rice

750 ml (1¼ pints) vegetable stock (see page 125 for homemade)

finely grated rind and juice of 1 lemon

2 spring onions, chopped

large handful of chopped parsley

½ red chilli, chopped

salt and pepper

—

**1** Heat the butter and oil in a large, heavy-based saucepan. Add the mushrooms and cook for 3 minutes until golden, then remove from the pan and set aside. Add the onion to the pan and cook for 5 minutes until softened, then stir in the garlic. Add the rice and stir until coated in the oil, then pour in the stock.

**2** Bring to the boil, then reduce the heat and simmer for about 15 minutes until most of the liquid has been absorbed. Return the mushrooms to the pan, cover and cook very gently for 5 minutes or until the rice is tender. Season to taste and stir in the remaining ingredients before serving.

# OVEN-BAKED SQUASH WITH QUINOA

LOW-GI FOR LONGER-LASTING ENERGY IN ADDITION TO BEING A COMPLETE PROTEIN, QUINOA IS A GREAT ALTERNATIVE TO STARCHY GRAINS.

—

**SERVES 4**

**PREP TIME** 10 minutes

**COOKING TIME** 40 minutes

—

2 tablespoons olive oil

750 g (1½ lb) butternut squash, peeled, deseeded and cut into 3.5 cm (1½ inch) chunks

25 g (1 oz) unsalted butter

1 red onion, chopped

1 garlic clove, crushed

50 g (2 oz) pine nuts

300 g (10 oz) quinoa

150 ml (¼ pint) dry white wine

1 cinnamon stick

1 litre (1¾ pints) vegetable stock (see page 125 for homemade)

4 tablespoons chopped mint

200 g (7 oz) feta cheese, crumbled

100 g (3½ oz) pomegranate seeds

salt and black pepper

**1** Heat the oil in a large frying pan and add the squash in a single layer. Season well with salt and pepper and cook over a medium heat for about 10 minutes until lightly browned.

**2** Meanwhile, melt the butter in a flameproof casserole dish, add the onion and garlic and cook for 2–3 minutes until softened. Stir in the pine nuts and quinoa and cook for 1 minute or until the quinoa is starting to pop. Add the wine and cook until it has been absorbed.

**3** Stir in the squash, cinnamon stick and stock. Bring to the boil, season to taste with salt and pepper and stir well.

**4** Cover the dish with the lid and cook in a preheated oven, 190°C (375°F), Gas Mark 5, for 25 minutes until the quinoa is just tender.

**5** Stir in the mint, then scatter over the feta and pomegranate seeds. Serve immediately.

# HEALTHY FATS

OUR BODIES NEED FAT FOR HEALTH BUT NOT ALL FATS ARE EQUAL. THE ONES TO INCLUDE IN YOUR DAILY DIET ARE MONOUNSATURATED AND POLYUNSATURATED FATS, WHICH YOU WILL FIND FEATURED IN THE MOUTHWATERING RECIPES IN THIS CHAPTER.

# BUCKWHEAT & SALMON SALAD

GOOD FOR YOUR BRAIN, HEART AND JOINTS, SALMON IS LOADED WITH OMEGA-3 FATS.

—

—

**SERVES 4**

**PREP TIME** 15 minutes

**COOKING TIME** 20 minutes

—

300 g (10 oz) buckwheat

250 g (8 oz) broccoli florets

250 g (8 oz) cherry tomatoes, halved

250 g (8 oz) smoked salmon

small bunch of parsley, chopped

4 tablespoons chopped dill salt and pepper

**DRESSING**

juice of 1 lemon

3 tablespoons olive oil

**1** Put the buckwheat in a saucepan, cover with cold water and add a pinch of salt. Bring to the boil and cook for 10–15 minutes until still firm and not mushy. Drain under running cold water and remove the foam that accumulates. Drain again when cool.

**2** Bring a large saucepan of lightly salted water to the boil and blanch the broccoli florets for 2–3 minutes. Refresh in cold water and drain.

**3** Mix the cherry tomatoes with the buckwheat and broccoli in a large salad bowl. Slice the smoked salmon and add it to the bowl with the parsley and half of the dill.

**4** Make the dressing by whisking the lemon juice and oil. Pour the dressing over the salad, mix lightly to combine and season to taste with salt and pepper. Serve immediately, garnished with the remaining dill.

# CHARRED LEEK SALAD WITH HAZELNUTS

CRUNCHY HAZELNUTS HAVE AN IMPRESSIVE STORE OF MONOUNSATURATED FAT, VITAMIN E AND MINERALS.

—

—

**SERVES 4**

**PREP TIME** 10 minutes

**COOKING TIME** 12–16 minutes

—

500 g (1 lb) baby leeks

1–2 tablespoons hazelnut oil

dash of lemon juice

40 g (1½ oz) blanched hazelnuts

2 Little Gem or cos lettuce hearts

a few sprigs of mint

15 g (½ oz) pecorino cheese

20 black olives, to garnish

**DRESSING**

4 tablespoons hazelnut oil

2 tablespoons extra-virgin olive oil

2 teaspoons sherry vinegar

salt and pepper

**1** Brush the leeks with the hazelnut oil. Cook, in batches, on a preheated hot ridged griddle pan or under a preheated hot grill, turning frequently, for 6–8 minutes until evenly browned and cooked through. Toss with the lemon juice and season with salt and pepper. Leave to cool.

**2** Heat a heavy-based frying pan until hot meanwhile, add the hazelnuts and cook over a medium heat, stirring, for 3–4 minutes until browned. Leave to cool slightly and then roughly chop. Separate the lettuce leaves and pull the mint leaves from the sprigs.

**3** Arrange the leeks in bowls and top with the lettuce leaves, mint and hazelnuts. Whisk all the dressing ingredients together in a small bowl, season with salt and pepper and pour over the salad. Shave the pecorino over the salad and serve garnished with the olives.

# SPICY SARDINE LINGUINE

FOR ALL-ROUND WELLBEING, WE SHOULD AIM TO EAT TWO PORTIONS OF OILY FISH, SUCH AS SARDINES, EVERY WEEK.

—

—

**SERVES 4**

**PREP TIME** 5 minutes

**COOKING TIME** 20 minutes

—

2 tablespoons olive oil

1 red onion, chopped

2 garlic cloves, crushed

400 g (13 oz) can cherry tomatoes

½ teaspoon dried chilli flakes

pinch of sugar

½ teaspoon finely grated lemon rind

350 g (11½ oz) linguine

2 x 120 g (3¾ oz) cans sardines in oil, drained

2 teaspoons rinsed capers

salt and pepper

basil leaves, to garnish (optional)

**1** Heat the olive oil in a large pan and cook the onion and garlic over a medium heat for 6–7 minutes, until softened. Add the tomatoes, chilli flakes, sugar, lemon rind and seasoning and bring to the boil. Cover and simmer for about 10 minutes, until thickened.

**2** Meanwhile, cook the linguine in a large pan of boiling salted water for 11 minutes, or according to the packet instructions, until 'al dente'. Drain, reserving 2 tablespoons of the cooking water and return to the pan.

**3** Stir the sardines and capers into the tomato sauce for the final 1–2 minutes. When hot, add to the drained pasta along with the reserved cooking water and toss gently. Serve heaped into bowls and garnished with extra black pepper, and with basil leaves, if desired.

# TROUT & CRACKED WHEAT SALAD

THIS IS A DOUBLE-WHAMMY DISH THAT HAS BOTH HEART-HEALTHY FISH AND NUTRITIOUS WHOLEGRAIN CRACKED WHEAT.

—

—

**SERVES 4**

**PREP TIME** 10 minutes, plus cooling

**COOKING TIME** 20 minutes

—

400 g (13 oz) cracked wheat

1 tablespoon olive oil

375 g (12 oz) smoked trout fillet, flaked

1 cucumber, deseeded and diced

150 g (5 oz) baby spinach leaves, washed

1 red onion, sliced

200 g (7 oz) can green lentils, rinsed and drained

75 g (3 oz) sugar snap peas, finely sliced

**LEMON & POPPY SEED DRESSING**

grated rind of 2 lemons

4 tablespoons lemon juice

2 tablespoons poppy seeds

2 tablespoons chopped dill

salt and pepper

**1** Cook the cracked wheat according to the instructions on the packet. Stir through the oil and set aside.

**2** Stir the trout into the cooled cracked wheat, then add the cucumber, spinach, red onion, lentils and peas.

**3** Make the dressing by mixing together the lemon rind and juice, poppy seeds and dill. Season the dressing to taste and just before serving drizzle it over the salad.

# CRISPY SALMON RAMEN

NOW POPULAR THE WORLD OVER, RAMEN IS A JAPANESE NOODLE SOUP DISH. THIS HEART-FRIENDLY VERSION INCLUDES SUPERFOOD SALMON.

—

**SERVES 2**

**PREP TIME** 15 minutes

**COOKING TIME** 15 minutes

—

2 teaspoons groundnut oil

2 boneless salmon fillets, skin on

500 ml (17 oz) hot clear chicken stock

1 tablespoon lime juice

2 teaspoons fish sauce

1 tablespoon soy sauce

1.5 cm (¾ inch) piece of fresh root ginger, peeled and cut into matchsticks

1 small red chilli, thinly sliced

2 heads of pak choi, sliced in half lengthways

150 g (5 oz) ramen or egg noodles

coriander leaves, to garnish

—

**1** Place the oil in a large frying pan over a medium heat and fry the salmon fillets, skin-side down, for 3–5 minutes, until the skin is really crispy. Turn carefully and cook for a further minute, until still slightly rare. Transfer to a plate and keep warm.

**2** Pour the stock into a saucepan, add the lime juice, fish sauce, soy sauce and ginger and bring to the boil. Simmer for 3–4 minutes, then add the chilli and pak choi and simmer for another 4–5 minutes, until tender.

**3** Meanwhile, cook the noodles in a pan of boiling water for 2–3 minutes, or according to the packet instructions, until just tender. Drain and heap into bowls.

**4** Ladle over the hot broth and top each bowl with a salmon fillet. Serve immediately, garnished with coriander leaves.

# MACKEREL & WILD RICE NIÇOISE

MACKEREL, LIKE ALL OILY FISH, IS RICH IN OILS, PLUS A VARIETY OF MINERALS AND VITAMINS. YOU COULD USE FRESH TUNA IN THIS DISH INSTEAD OF THE MACKEREL.

—

**SERVES 3–4**

**PREP TIME** 20 minutes, plus cooling

**COOKING TIME** 25 minutes

—

100 g (3½ oz) wild rice

150 g (5 oz) French beans, topped and tailed, then halved

300 g (10 oz) large mackerel fillets, pin-boned

90 ml (3½ fl oz) olive oil

12 black olives

8 canned anchovy fillets, drained and halved

250 g (8 oz) cherry tomatoes, halved

3 hard-boiled eggs, cut into quarters

1 tablespoon lemon juice

1 tablespoon French mustard

2 tablespoons chopped chives

salt and pepper

**1** Cook the rice in plenty of boiling water for 20–25 minutes until tender. (The grains will start to split open when they are just cooked.) Add the French beans and cook for another 2 minutes.

**2** Lay the mackerel, skin side up, on a foil-lined grill rack, while the rice is cooking. Brush with 1 tablespoon of the oil and cook under a preheated medium-hot grill for 8–10 minutes, turning after the first 5 minutes, until cooked through; the second side should not take as long to cook as the first. Leave to cool.

**3** Drain the rice and beans and mix together in a salad bowl with the olives, anchovies, tomatoes and eggs. Flake the mackerel, discarding any stray bones, and add to the bowl.

**4** Whisk the remaining oil with the lemon juice, French mustard and chives in a small bowl, and season with a little salt and pepper. Add to the bowl.

**5** Toss the ingredients together lightly, cover and chill until ready to serve.

# PORK, APPLE & GINGER STIR-FRY

THIS RECIPE USES COCONUT OIL – WHICH INCREASES GOOD CHOLESTEROL AND PROMOTES A HEALTHY HEART – FOR STIR-FRYING.

—

**SERVES 4**

**PREP TIME** 15 minutes

**COOKING TIME** 15 minutes

—

2 tablespoons sesame seeds

1 tablespoon coconut oil

300 g (10 oz) pork fillet, in strips

2 garlic cloves, chopped

5-cm (2-inch) fresh root ginger, peeled and cut into matchsticks

1 green chilli, deseeded and chopped

2 apples, cored and cut into wedges

2 carrots, cut into matchsticks

150 g (5 oz) broccoli florets

300 g (10 oz) ribbon rice noodles

juice of 1 lime

—

**1** Heat a nonstick frying pan over a medium-low heat and dry-fry the sesame seeds for 2 minutes, stirring frequently, until golden and toasted. Set aside.

**2** Heat the oil in a wok or large frying pan, add the pork and stir-fry for 6–8 minutes, until lightly browned. Add the garlic, ginger, chilli, apples and vegetables and stir-fry for a further 4–5 minutes or until the pork is cooked through.

**3** Meanwhile, cook the noodles according to the pack instructions, then add to the stir-fry with the lime juice and toss all the ingredients together.

**4** Serve sprinkled with the toasted sesame seeds.

# VEGETABLE, FRUIT & NUT BIRYANI

RESEARCH SHOWS THAT, AS WELL AS BEING CHOCK-FULL OF GOOD FATS, CASHEW NUTS CAN HELP TO FIGHT AGAINST DIABETES AND CANCER.

—

**SERVES 4**

**PREP TIME** 15 minutes

**COOKING TIME** 20 minutes

—

250 g (8 oz) basmati rice

½ cauliflower, broken into florets

2 tablespoons vegetable oil

2 large sweet potatoes, peeled and cut into cubes

1 large onion, sliced

3 tablespoons hot curry paste

½ teaspoon ground turmeric

2 teaspoons mustard seeds

300 ml (½ pint) hot vegetable stock (see page 125 for homemade)

250 g (8 oz) fine green beans, halved

100 g (3½ oz) sultanas

6 tablespoons chopped fresh coriander

50 g (2 oz) cashew nuts, lightly toasted

—

**1** Bring a large saucepan of lightly salted water to the boil and cook the rice for 5 minutes. Add the cauliflower and cook with the rice for a further 10 minutes or until both are tender, then drain.

**2** Meanwhile, heat the oil in a large, heavy-based frying pan and cook the sweet potatoes and onion over a medium heat, stirring occasionally, for 10 minutes, until browned and tender. Add the curry paste, turmeric and mustard seeds and cook, stirring, for a further 2 minutes.

**3** Pour in the stock and add the green beans. Bring to the boil, then reduce the heat and simmer for 5 minutes.

**4** Stir in the drained rice and cauliflower, sultanas, coriander and cashew nuts and simmer for a further 2 minutes. Serve with poppadums and raita.

# BEETROOT, WALNUT & BUTTERNUT SQUASH SPAGHETTI

THE WALNUTS IN THIS DISH ARE AN EXCELLENT VEGETARIAN SOURCE OF OMEGA-3 FATTY ACIDS, WHILE THE FATTY ACIDS AND ANTIOXIDANTS IN OLIVE OIL HAVE POWERFUL HEALTH BENEFITS.

—

**SERVES 4**

**PREP TIME** 8 minutes

**COOKING TIME** 10 minutes

—

300 g (10 oz) dried spaghetti or fusilli

150 g (5 oz) fine green beans

500 g (1 lb) butternut squash, peeled, deseeded and cut into 1 cm (½ inch) dice

4 tablespoons olive oil

500 g (1 lb) raw beetroot, cut into 1 cm (½ inch) dice

50 g (2 oz) walnuts, crushed

150 g (5 oz) goats' cheese, diced

2 tablespoons lemon juice

freshly grated Parmesan cheese, to serve (optional)

—

**1** Cook the pasta in lightly salted boiling water for 10 minutes or until just cooked. Add the beans and squash for the final 2 minutes of cooking time.

**2** Meanwhile, heat the oil in a large frying pan, add the beetroot and cook, stirring occasionally, for 10 minutes, until cooked but still firm.

**3** Toss the drained pasta mixture with the beetroot, walnuts and goats' cheese. Squeeze over the lemon juice and serve immediately with a bowl of Parmesan, if desired.

# BEAN CHILLI WITH AVOCADO SALSA

THE SALSA THAT TOPS THIS HEARTY VEGGIE CHILLI INCLUDES AVOCADO, WHICH IS RICH IN MONOUNSATURATED FATS AND VITAMIN E.

—

**SERVES 4–6**

**PREP TIME** 15 minutes

**COOKING TIME** 30 minutes

—

3 tablespoons olive oil

2 teaspoons cumin seeds, crushed

1 teaspoon dried oregano

1 red onion, chopped

1 celery stick, chopped

1 red chilli, deseeded and sliced

2 x 400 g (13 oz) cans chopped tomatoes

50 g (2 oz) sun-dried tomatoes, thinly sliced

2 teaspoons sugar

300 ml (½ pint) vegetable stock (see page 125 for homemade)

2 x 400 g (13 oz) cans red kidney beans, drained

handful of coriander, chopped

100 g (3½ oz) low-fat soured cream

salt and pepper

**SALSA**

1 small avocado

2 tomatoes

2 tablespoons sweet chilli sauce

2 teaspoons lime juice

**1** Heat the oil in a large saucepan over a medium-low heat, add the cumin seeds, oregano, onion, celery and chilli and cook gently, stirring frequently, for about 6–8 minutes or until the vegetables are beginning to colour.

**2** Add the canned tomatoes, sun-dried tomatoes, sugar, stock, red kidney beans and coriander and bring to the boil. Reduce the heat and simmer for about 20 minutes or until the juices are thickened and pulpy.

**3** Make the salsa. Peel, stone and finely dice the avocado and put it in a small bowl. Halve the tomatoes, scoop out the seeds and finely dice the flesh. Add to the bowl along with the chilli sauce and lime juice. Mix well.

**4** Season the bean mixture with salt and pepper and spoon into bowls. Top with spoonfuls of soured cream and the avocado salsa. Serve with toasted pitta or flatbreads.

# NOURISHING

THE RECIPES IN THIS CHAPTER USE GREAT-TASTING VEGETABLES
IN A RAINBOW OF COLOURS, PLUS WHOLESOME PULSES, BEANS, LEAN
PROTEIN AND GRAINS TO GIVE MAXIMUM HEALTH BENEFITS.

# PESTO & LEMON SOUP

THE BROCCOLI IN THIS LOVELY SOUP IS A POWERHOUSE OF NUTRIENTS FROM VITAMIN A TO ZINC, WHILE THE SPINACH, LIKE ALL LEAFY GREENS, IS ESSENTIAL FOR HEALTHY SKIN, HAIR AND BONES.

—

**SERVES 6**

**PREP TIME** 10 minutes

**COOKING TIME** 25 minutes

—

1 tablespoon olive oil

1 onion, finely chopped

2 garlic cloves, finely chopped

2 tomatoes, skinned, chopped

1.2 litres (2 pints) vegetable stock (see page 125 for homemade)

3 teaspoons pesto, plus extra to serve

grated rind and juice of 1 lemon

100 g (3½ oz) broccoli, cut into small florets, stems sliced

150 g (5 oz) courgettes, diced

100 g (3½ oz) frozen green soya beans

65 g (2½ oz) small pasta shapes

50 g (2 oz) spinach, shredded

salt and pepper

fresh basil leaves, to garnish (optional)

—

**1** Heat the oil in a saucepan, add the onion and fry gently for 5 minutes, stirring occasionally, until softened. Add the garlic, tomatoes, stock, pesto, lemon rind and a little salt and pepper and simmer gently for 10 minutes.

**2** Add the broccoli, courgettes, soya beans and pasta shapes, then simmer for 6 minutes. Add the spinach and lemon juice and cook for 2 minutes until the spinach has just wilted and the pasta is cooked.

**3** Ladle into bowls, top with extra spoonfuls of pesto and garnish with a sprinkling of basil leaves. Serve with warm focaccia or ciabatta bread.

# KALE SOUP WITH GARLIC CROUTONS

DUBBED 'THE QUEEN OF GREENS', KALE CONTAINS ANTIOXIDANTS, VITAMINS, FOLIATES, MAGNESIUM AND FIBRE.

—

**SERVES 8**

**PREP TIME** 25 minutes

**COOKING TIME** 45 minutes

—

50 g (2 oz) butter

1 onion, chopped

2 carrots, sliced

500 g (1 lb) kale, tough stalks discarded

1.2 litres (2 pints) water

600 ml (1 pint) vegetable stock (see page 125 for homemade)

1 tablespoon lemon juice

300 g (10 oz) potatoes, sliced

pinch of grated nutmeg

salt and pepper

2 kale leaves, thinly shredded, to garnish

## GARLIC CROUTONS

90–125 ml (3½–4 fl oz) olive oil

3 garlic cloves, sliced

6-8 slices wholemeal bread, crusts removed, cut into 1 cm (½ inch) cubes

**1** Melt the butter in a large saucepan, add the onion and cook over a medium heat for 5 minutes or until soft. Add the carrots and kale in batches, stirring constantly. Cook for 2 minutes, until the kale has just wilted.

**2** Pour in the measured water and stock, then add the lemon juice, potatoes and nutmeg. Season with salt and pepper. Bring to the boil, then reduce the heat, cover and simmer for 30–35 minutes, until all the vegetables are tender. Add a little water if the soup is too thick.

**3** Make the croutons while the soup is cooking. Heat the oil in a large frying pan, add the garlic and cook over a medium heat for 1 minute. Add the bread cubes and cook, turning frequently, until golden brown. Remove with a slotted spoon and drain on kitchen paper. Remove and discard the garlic. Add the shredded kale to the pan and cook, stirring constantly, until crispy.

**4** Reheat the soup gently. Serve in bowls, garnished with the croutons and crispy shredded kale.

# CHICKEN WITH SPRING VEGETABLES

THIS APPETIZING DISH COMBINES CHICKEN FOR PROTEIN PLUS AN IMPRESSIVE ARRAY OF VITAMINS AND MINERALS FROM THE DELICIOUS VEGETABLES AND HERBS.

—

—

**SERVES 4**

**PREP TIME** 10 minutes, plus resting

**COOKING TIME** about 1¼ hours

—

1.5 kg (3 lb) chicken

about 1.5 litres (2½ pints) hot chicken stock

2 shallots, halved

2 garlic cloves

2 sprigs of parsley

2 sprigs of marjoram

2 sprigs of lemon thyme

2 carrots, halved

1 leek, trimmed and sliced

200 g (7 oz) tenderstem broccoli

250 g (8 oz) asparagus, trimmed

½ Savoy cabbage, shredded

**1** Put the chicken in a large saucepan and pour over enough stock just to cover the chicken. Add the shallots, garlic, herbs, carrots and leek to the pan and place over a medium-high heat. Bring to the boil, then reduce the heat and simmer gently for 1 hour or until the chicken is falling away from the bones.

**2** Add the remaining vegetables to the pan and simmer for a further 6–8 minutes or until the vegetables are cooked.

**3** Turn off the heat and leave to rest for 5–10 minutes before serving the chicken and vegetables in bowls with spoonfuls of the broth. Remove the skin, if preferred, and serve with plenty of crusty bread.

# FRAGRANT VIETNAMESE BEEF CURRY

INTENSELY FLAVOURED FISH SAUCE – USUALLY MADE WITH ANCHOVIES AND SALT – SHOULD BE USED SPARINGLY.

—

**SERVES 4**

**PREP TIME** 15 minutes

**COOKING TIME** 20–25
   minutes

—

2 tablespoons groundnut oil

750 g (1½ lb) thin-cut fillet
   steak, cut into strips

1 onion, finely sliced

4 garlic cloves, crushed

1 fresh red chilli, finely sliced

2 star anise

1 teaspoon cardamom
   seeds, crushed

1 cinnamon stick

300 g (10 oz) French beans,
   trimmed

1 carrot, cut into batons

2 tablespoons Thai fish
   sauce

2 tablespoons ground bean
   sauce

**TO GARNISH**

small handful of finely
   chopped coriander leaves

small handful of finely
   chopped mint leaves

**1** Heat half the oil in a large nonstick frying pan and stir-fry the beef in batches for 1–2 minutes. Remove with a slotted spoon and keep warm.

**2** Heat the remaining oil in the frying pan and stir-fry the onion for 4–5 minutes until softened, then add the garlic, chilli, star anise, cardamom, cinnamon, French beans and carrot. Stir-fry for 6–8 minutes.

**3** Return the beef to the pan with the fish sauce and ground bean sauce. Stir-fry for 3–4 minutes or until heated through. Remove from the heat and sprinkle over the chopped herbs just before serving.

# PRAWN, PEA SHOOT & QUINOA SALAD

DELICATELY FLAVOURED PEA SHOOTS ARE THE LEAVES OF THE PEA PLANT AND ARE PACKED WITH VITAMINS A, C AND FOLIC ACID.

—

—

**SERVES 4**

**PREP TIME** 10 minutes

**COOKING TIME** 10 minutes

—

300 g (10 oz) quinoa

75 g (3 oz) mangetout, blanched and halved

200 g (7 oz) asparagus spears, cooked, cooled and cut into bite-sized pieces

50 g (2 oz) pea shoots

400 g (13 oz) cooked tiger prawns, shells removed

salt and pepper

**FRUIT & NUT DRESSING**

2 tablespoons olive oil

2 tablespoons lemon juice

20 g (¾ oz) dried cranberries

50 g (2 oz) hazelnuts, chopped and toasted

**1** Cook the quinoa according to the instructions on the packet. Set aside to cool.

**2** Stir the mangetout and asparagus through the quinoa. Make the dressing by mixing together the oil, lemon juice, cranberries and hazelnuts.

**3** Spoon the pea shoots and prawns over the quinoa, drizzle over the dressing and serve.

# VEGETABLE & TOFU STIR-FRY

LOW CALORIE AND GLUTEN FREE, TOFU, WHICH IS MADE FROM SOYA BEANS, IS AN EXCELLENT VEGETARIAN SOURCE OF PROTEIN, IRON AND MINERALS.

—

**SERVES 4**

**PREP TIME** 10 minutes

**COOKING TIME** 7 minutes

—

3 tablespoons sunflower oil

300 g (10 oz) firm tofu, cubed

1 onion, sliced

2 carrots, sliced

150 g (5 oz) broccoli, broken into small florets and stalks sliced

1 red pepper, cored, deseeded and sliced

1 large courgette, sliced

150 g (5 oz) sugar snap peas

2 tablespoons soy sauce

2 tablespoons sweet chilli sauce

125 ml (4 fl oz) water

**TO GARNISH**

chopped red chillies

Thai or ordinary basil leaves

**1** Heat 1 tablespoon of the oil in a wok or large frying pan until starting to smoke, add the tofu and stir-fry over a high heat for 2 minutes or until golden. Remove with a slotted spoon and keep warm.

**2** Heat the remaining oil in the pan, add the onion and carrots and stir-fry for 1½ minutes. Add the broccoli and red pepper and stir-fry for 1 minute, then add the courgette and sugar snap peas and stir-fry for 1 minute.

**3** Mix together the soy sauce, chilli sauce and measured water and add to the pan with the tofu. Cook for 1 minute. Serve in bowls, garnished with chopped red chillies and basil leaves.

# RED PEPPER & SPINACH STEW

THE BONE-BUILDING KIDNEY BEANS IN THIS COLOURFUL STEW ARE ALSO SUPERCHARGED WITH ANTIOXIDANTS, FIBRE AND PROTEIN.

—

**SERVES 4**

**PREP TIME** 10 minutes

**COOKING TIME** 20 minutes

—

3 tablespoons olive or vegetable oil

2 large red peppers, cored, deseeded and cut into large pieces

3 garlic cloves, sliced

2 teaspoons ground cumin or Mexican spice mix, such as fajita seasoning (optional)

2 tablespoons tomato purée

400 ml (14 fl oz) hot vegetable stock (see page 125 for homemade)

400 g (13 oz) can chopped tomatoes

610 g (1 lb 3¾ oz) canned kidney beans, rinsed and drained

200 g (7 oz) frozen leaf spinach, defrosted and drained

salt and pepper

—

**1** Heat the oil in a saucepan and cook the peppers and garlic over a medium heat for 5–6 minutes, stirring frequently, until softened.

**2** Stir in the cumin or Mexican spice of choice, if using, and cook for 1 minute before adding the tomato purée, hot stock, chopped tomatoes and kidney beans. Bring to the boil, season to taste, then cover and simmer gently for 10–12 minutes until thickened slightly. Stir in the spinach for the final minute of cooking, then ladle into bowls to serve.

# CURRIED CAULIFLOWER WITH CHICKPEAS

AMONG ITS MANY HEALTH BENEFITS, ONE SERVING OF CAULIFLOWER CONTAINS 77 PER CENT OF YOUR RECOMMENDED DAILY INTAKE OF VITAMIN C.

—

**SERVES** 4

**PREP TIME** 10 minutes

**COOKING TIME** 20 minutes

—

2 tablespoons olive oil

1 onion, chopped

2 garlic cloves, crushed

4 tablespoons medium curry paste

1 small cauliflower, divided into florets

375 ml (13 fl oz) vegetable stock (see page 125 for homemade)

4 tomatoes, roughly chopped

400 g (13 oz) canned chickpeas, rinsed and drained

2 tablespoons mango chutney

salt and pepper

4 tablespoons chopped coriander, to garnish.

—

**1** Heat the oil in a saucepan, add the onion and garlic and cook until the onion is soft and starting to brown. Stir in the curry paste, add the cauliflower and stock and bring to the boil. Reduce the heat, cover tightly and simmer for 10 minutes.

**2** Add the tomatoes, chickpeas and mango chutney and continue to cook, uncovered, for 10 minutes. Season to taste with salt and pepper. Garnish with coriander and serve with rolled chapatis, if desired.

# MALAYSIAN COCONUT VEGETABLES

THE PULP OF THE SOUR TAMARIND FRUIT ADDS A DISTINCTIVE FLAVOUR TO MANY SOUTH-EAST ASIAN DISHES.

—

**SERVES 4**

**PREP TIME** 15 minutes, plus soaking

**COOKING TIME** 20 minutes

—

125 g (4 oz) broccoli florets

125 g (4 oz) French beans, cut into 2.5 cm (1 inch) lengths

1 red pepper, cored, deseeded and sliced

125 g (4 oz) courgettes, thinly sliced

COCONUT SAUCE

25 g (1 oz) tamarind pulp

150 ml (¼ pint) boiling water

400 ml (14 fl oz) can coconut milk

2 teaspoons Thai green curry paste

1 teaspoon grated fresh root ginger

1 onion, cut into small cubes

½ teaspoon ground turmeric

salt

**1** Make the coconut sauce. Put the tamarind in a bowl. Pour over the measured water and leave to soak for 30 minutes. Mash the tamarind in the water, then push through a sieve set over another bowl, squashing the tamarind so that you get as much of the pulp as possible; discard the stringy bits and any seeds.

**2** Take 2 tablespoons of the cream from the top of the coconut milk and pour it into a wok or large frying pan. Add the Thai curry paste, ginger, onion and turmeric, and cook over a gentle heat, stirring, for 2–3 minutes. Stir in the rest of the coconut milk and the tamarind water. Bring to the boil, then reduce the heat to a simmer and add a pinch of salt.

**3** Add the broccoli to the coconut sauce and cook for 5 minutes, then add the green beans and red pepper. Cook, stirring, for another 5 minutes. Finally, stir in the courgettes and cook gently for 1–2 minutes, until the courgette is just tender. Serve immediately with some crispy prawn crackers.

# CHICKPEA & AUBERGINE TAGINE

USED EXTENSIVELY IN NORTH AFRICAN COOKING, PRESERVED LEMONS ARE WHOLE LEMONS PRESERVED IN SALT, LEMON JUICE AND OIL.

—

**SERVES 4**

**PREP TIME** 10 minutes

**COOKING TIME** 45 minutes

—

1 tablespoon sunflower oil

1 large onion, sliced

2 garlic cloves, crushed

1 teaspoon ground cumin

1 teaspoon ground cinnamon

1 teaspoon ground turmeric

1 teaspoon ground paprika

2 aubergines, chopped into 3.5 cm (1½ inch) chunks

2 carrots, sliced

125 g (4 oz) soft dried pitted dates

400 g (13 oz) can chopped tomatoes

400 g (13 oz) can chickpeas, drained and rinsed

600 ml (1 pint) vegetable stock (see page 125 for homemade)

4 slices of preserved lemon

2 tablespoons chopped flat leaf parsley

salt and black pepper

couscous, to serve

—

**1** Heat the oil in a large saucepan, add the onion and garlic and cook over a medium heat for 4–5 minutes, until softened. Stir in all the spices and cook, stirring, for 1 minute.

**2** Add the aubergines and cook for about 5 minutes, until starting to soften. Stir in all the remaining ingredients, except the parsley, and season to taste with salt and pepper.

**3** Bring to the boil, then reduce the heat, cover and simmer for 30 minutes, stirring occasionally.

**4** Stir in the parsley, then serve in bowls with couscous.

# GOOD FOR YOUR GUT

THE RECIPES IN THIS CHAPTER ARE FULL OF INGREDIENTS TO HELP KEEP YOUR TUMMY HEALTHY AND MAKE YOU FEEL BETTER THAN EVER, INCLUDING PROBIOTICS, SOOTHING HERBS AND SPICES AND FIBRE-RICH FRUIT AND VEGETABLES.

# GREEN BEAN, MISO & NOODLE SOUP

MISO PASTE, WHICH IS MADE FROM FERMENTED SOYA BEANS, IS BRIMMING WITH GUT-FRIENDLY PROBIOTICS.

**SERVES 2**

**PREP TIME** 10 minutes

**COOKING TIME** 10 minutes

—

3 tablespoons brown miso paste

1 litre (1¾ pints) vegetable stock (see page 125 for homemade)

25 g (1 oz) fresh root ginger, peeled and grated

2 garlic cloves, thinly sliced

1 small hot red chilli, deseeded and thinly sliced

100 g (3½ oz) dried soba, wholemeal or plain noodles

1 bunch of spring onions, finely shredded

100 g (3½ oz) fresh or frozen peas

250 g (8 oz) runner beans, trimmed and shredded

3 tablespoons mirin

1 tablespoon sugar

1 tablespoon rice wine vinegar

**1** Blend the miso paste with a little of the stock in a saucepan to make a thick, smooth paste. Add a little more stock to thin the paste and then pour in the remainder. Add the ginger, garlic and chilli and bring almost to the boil.

**2** Reduce the heat to a gentle simmer, add the noodles, stirring until they have softened into the stock, and cook for about 5 minutes or until the noodles are just tender.

**3** Add the spring onions, peas, runner beans, mirin, sugar and rice wine vinegar and stir well.

**4** Cook gently for 1–2 minutes or until the vegetables have softened. Ladle into bowls and serve immediately.

# CRAB & GRAPEFRUIT SALAD

AS WELL AS TOPPING UP VITAMIN-C LEVELS, THE FIBRE IN CITRUS IS IMPORTANT FOR OVERALL DIGESTIVE HEALTH.

—

—

**SERVES 4**

**PREP TIME** 10 minutes

—

400 g (13 oz) white crab meat

1 pink grapefruit, peeled and sliced

50 g (2 oz) rocket

3 spring onions, sliced

200 g (7 oz) mangetout, halved

salt and pepper

**WATERCRESS DRESSING**

85 g (3¼ oz) watercress, tough stalks removed

1 tablespoon Dijon mustard

2 tablespoon olive oil

**TO SERVE**

4 chapattis

lime wedges

**1** Combine the crab meat, grapefruit, rocket, spring onions and mangetout in a serving dish. Season to taste.

**2** Make the dressing by blending together the watercress, mustard and oil. Season with salt.

**3** Toast the chapattis. Stir the dressing into the salad and serve with the toasted chapattis and lime wedges on the side.

# BULGAR WHEAT SALAD

LOW IN FAT AND HIGH IN MINERALS, BULGAR WHEAT ALSO PROVIDES A HEFTY HELPING OF DIETARY FIBRE.

—

**SERVES 4**

**PREP TIME** 10 minutes

**COOKING TIME** 20 minutes

—

750 ml (1¼ pints) hot vegetable stock (see page 125 for homemade)

275 g (9 oz) bulgar wheat

4 tablespoons olive or vegetable oil

1 large red onion, halved and thinly sliced

100 ml (3½ fl oz) tomato juice

2 tablespoons lime juice

175 g (6 oz) firm goats' cheese, crumbled

3 tablespoons roughly chopped flat leaf parsley

salt and pepper

—

**1** Bring the vegetable stock to the boil in a large saucepan, add the bulgar wheat and cook for 7 minutes. Remove from the heat, cover with a tight-fitting lid and set aside for 5–8 minutes, until the liquid has been absorbed and the grains are tender.

**2** Meanwhile, heat 2 tablespoons of oil in a frying pan and cook the onion gently for 7–8 minutes, until soft and golden.

**3** Combine the remaining oil with the tomato juice and lime juice, and season with salt and pepper. Fold the dressing, onion, goats' cheese and parsley into the bulgar wheat with a fork, and spoon into bowls to serve.

# THAI MUSSEL CURRY WITH GINGER & LEMONGRASS

LEMONGRASS HAS A SWEET, LEMONY FLAVOUR AND IS KEY TO THAI COOKING. IT IS A GOOD AID TO DIGESTION, TOO.

—

**SERVES 4**

**PREP TIME** 30 minutes

**COOKING TIME** 13 minutes

—

½–1 large red chilli (to taste)

2 shallots, quartered

1 lemongrass stem

2.5 cm (1 inch) piece of fresh root ginger, peeled and chopped

1 tablespoon sunflower oil

400 ml (14 fl oz) can reduced-fat coconut milk

4–5 kaffir lime leaves

150 ml (¼ pint) fish stock

2 teaspoons Thai fish sauce

1.5 kg (3 lb) fresh mussels, soaked in cold water

small bunch of coriander, torn into pieces, to garnish

—

**1** Halve the chilli and keep the seeds for extra heat, if desired. Put the chilli, shallots and lemongrass into a liquidizer goblet with the ginger and process together until finely chopped.

**2** Heat the oil in large, deep saucepan, add the finely chopped ingredients and fry over a medium heat for 5 minutes, stirring, until softened. Add the coconut milk, kaffir lime leaves, fish stock and Thai fish sauce and cook for 3 minutes. Set aside until ready to finish.

**3** Meanwhile, pick over the mussels and discard any that are opened or have cracked shells. Scrub with a small nailbrush, remove any barnacles and pull off the small, hairy beards. Put them in a bowl of clean water and leave until ready to cook.

**4** Reheat the coconut milk mixture. Drain the mussels and add to the mixture. Cover the pan with a lid and cook for about 5 minutes until the mussel shells have opened.

**5** Spoon the mussels and the coconut sauce into bowls, discarding any mussels that have not opened. Garnish with the coriander.

# BEEF GOULASH

THE STRONGLY AROMATIC CARAWAY SEEDS USED IN THIS RICHLY SATISFYING GOULASH HAVE STOMACH-SOOTHING PROPERTIES.

—

**SERVES 8**

**PREP TIME** 10 minutes

**COOKING TIME** 2–2½ hours

—

1.5 kg (3 lb) braising steak

4 tablespoons olive oil

2 onions, sliced

2 red peppers, cored, deseeded and diced

1 tablespoon smoked paprika

2 tablespoons chopped marjoram

1 teaspoon caraway seeds

1 litre (1¾ pints) beef stock

5 tablespoons tomato purée

salt and pepper

French bread, to serve

—

**1** Cut the beef into large chunks. Heat the oil in a flameproof casserole and fry the beef in batches, until browned on all sides, lifting out with a slotted spoon on to a plate.

**2** Add the onions and red peppers to the casserole and cook gently for 10 minutes, until softened. Stir in the paprika, marjoram and caraway seeds and cook, stirring, for 1 minute.

**3** Return the beef to the casserole, add the beef stock, tomato purée and salt and pepper to taste and bring to the boil, stirring. Reduce the heat, cover and cook gently for 1½–2 hours. If the sauce needs thickening, uncover for the final 30 minutes. Serve with French bread.

# YOGURT CHICKEN WITH GREEK SALAD

THE PROBIOTICS IN YOGURT CONTAIN GOOD-FOR-YOU BACTERIA TO KEEP YOUR TUMMY IN TIP-TOP SHAPE.

—

—

**SERVES 4**

**PREP TIME** 10 minutes

**COOKING TIME** 10 minutes

—

150 g (5 oz) fat-free Greek yogurt

1 garlic clove, crushed

2 tablespoons olive oil

finely grated rind and juice of 1 lemon

1 teaspoon ground cumin

4 boneless, skinless chicken breasts, cut into bite-sized chunks

200 g (7 oz) cucumber, chopped

1 red onion, sliced

4 tomatoes, cut into slim wedges

16 black olives

175 g (6 oz) feta cheese, crumbled

1 small cos (romaine) lettuce, torn

### DRESSING

1 tablespoon lemon juice

2 tablespoons olive oil

1 tablespoon chopped fresh oregano or ½ teaspoon dried oregano

**1** Soak 8 small wooden skewers in water and preheat the grill to high. In a bowl, mix together the Greek yogurt, garlic, olive oil, lemon rind and juice and cumin. Add the chicken, stir well and then thread on to 8 skewers. Place on a foil-lined grill pan.

**2** Cook under a preheated hot grill for 10 minutes, turning occasionally, until the chicken is cooked and beginning to char in places.

**3** Meanwhile, in a salad bowl mix together the cucumber, onion, tomatoes, olives, feta and lettuce.

**4** Make the dressing by whisking together the lemon juice, oil and fresh or dried oregano. Pour the dressing over the salad and lightly mix together. Serve with the chicken skewers.

# QUICK GARLICKY TOMATO LENTILS

FAST FOOD DOESN'T NEED TO BE JUNK FOOD AS THIS SUPER-FAST, SUPER-FULL-OF-FIBRE DISH PROVES.

—

**SERVES 4**

**PREP TIME** 5 minutes

**COOKING TIME** 10 minutes

—

2 tablespoons olive or vegetable oil

1 large onion, chopped

2 garlic cloves, chopped

440 g (14¼ oz) jar tomato-based pasta sauce

1 teaspoon dried oregano or mixed herbs (optional)

2 x 390 g (12½ oz) cans green lentils, rinsed and drained

100 g (3½ oz) grated Cheddar cheese, Parmesan cheese or other hard Italian cheese (optional)

crusty bread, to serve

—

**1** Heat the oil in a large frying pan and cook the onion and garlic over a medium heat for 6–7 minutes, stirring frequently, until softened. Add the pasta sauce, dried oregano or mixed herbs, if using, and lentils and heat to simmering point.

**2** Spoon into bowls. Scatter with grated cheese, if using, and serve immediately with crusty bread.

# MOROCCAN VEGETABLE TAGINE

FIERY HARISSA IS A NORTH AFRICAN PASTE MADE FROM DRIED RED CHILLIES, GARLIC, OLIVE OIL AND A VARIETY OF SPICES.

—

**SERVES 4**

**PREP TIME** 15 minutes

**COOKING TIME** 30 minutes

—

200 g (7 oz) couscous

550 ml (18 fl oz) boiling water

2 tablespoons sunflower oil

1 large onion, finely chopped

2 garlic cloves, minced

1 teaspoon grated fresh root ginger

2 teaspoons ground cumin

1 teaspoon ground coriander

2 teaspoons ground cinnamon

1 teaspoon ground turmeric

2 teaspoons dried red chilli flakes

1 tablespoon harissa paste

400 g (13 oz) can chopped tomatoes

250 ml (8 fl oz) hot vegetable stock (see page 125 for homemade)

2 red peppers, cored, deseeded and cut into bite-sized pieces

700 g (1½ lb) butternut squash, peeled, deseeded and cubed

100 g (3½ oz) golden sultanas

salt and pepper

chopped fresh coriander, to garnish

**1** Put the couscous in a large heatproof bowl and season with salt. Pour over the measured water, cover with cling film and leave to stand for 10 minutes, or according to the pack instructions, until the water is absorbed. Gently fork to separate the grains, then set aside and keep warm.

**2** Meanwhile, heat the oil in a large frying pan, add the onion and cook over a medium heat, stirring occasionally, for 2–3 minutes, until softened. Add the garlic, ginger, ground spices, chilli flakes, harissa paste, tomatoes and stock and bring to the boil, then reduce the heat to low, cover and simmer gently for 10–12 minutes.

**3** Stir in the red peppers, squash and golden sultanas, re-cover and increase the heat to medium. Simmer for 10–15 minutes or until the vegetables are tender, then season to taste.

**4** Spoon the couscous into bowls, then ladle over the tagine and serve scattered with chopped coriander.

# GINGER RICE NOODLES

GINGER HAS LONG BEEN RECOGNIZED AS GOOD FOR YOUR GUT, AIDING DIGESTION AND REDUCING BLOATING.

—

**SERVES 4**

**PREP TIME** 10 minutes

**COOKING TIME** 5 minutes

—

100 g (3½ oz) fine rice noodles

125 g (4 oz) green beans, halved

50 g (2 oz) dried pineapple pieces, chopped

**DRESSING**

finely grated rind and juice of 2 limes

1 Thai chilli, deseeded and finely chopped

2.5 cm (1 inch) piece of fresh root ginger, peeled and finely chopped

2 teaspoons caster sugar

small handful of fresh coriander leaves, chopped

—

**1** Place the noodles in a bowl, cover with plenty of boiling water and leave for 4 minutes, until soft.

**2** Meanwhile, cook the beans in boiling water for about 3 minutes, until tender. Drain.

**3** To make the dressing, mix together the lime rind and juice, Thai chilli, ginger, caster sugar and coriander in a small bowl.

**4** Drain the noodles and place in a large bowl. Add the cooked beans, pineapple and dressing and toss together lightly before serving.

# ASPARAGUS & MANGETOUT STIR-FRY

RICH IN FIBRE BUT EASY TO DIGEST, ASPARAGUS WILL DECREASE BLOATING AT THE SAME TIME AS PROVIDING YOU WITH VITAMINS A, C, E, K AND CHROMIUM.

—

**SERVES 4**

**PREP TIME** 10 minutes

**COOKING TIME** 7–9 minutes

—

2 tablespoons vegetable oil

100 g (3½ oz) fresh root ginger, peeled and thinly shredded

2 large garlic cloves, thinly sliced

4 spring onions, diagonally sliced

250 g (8 oz) thin asparagus spears, cut into 3 cm (1¼ inch) lengths

150 g (5 oz) mangetout, cut in half diagonally

150 g (5 oz) bean sprouts

3 tablespoons light soy sauce

**TO SERVE**

steamed rice

extra soy sauce (optional)

—

**1** Heat a large wok until it is smoking then add the oil. Stir-fry the ginger and garlic for 30 seconds, add the spring onions and cook for a further 30 seconds. Add the asparagus and cook, stirring frequently, for another 3–4 minutes.

**2** Add the mangetout and cook for 2–3 minutes, until the vegetables are still crunchy but beginning to soften. Finally, add the bean sprouts and toss in the hot oil for 1–2 minutes before pouring in the soy sauce and removing from the heat.

**3** Serve immediately with steamed rice and extra soy sauce, if desired.

# RAW FOODS

A FABULOUS ARRAY OF COLOURFUL, TASTY AND NOURISHING NON-COOK AND BARELY-COOK BOWLS THAT MAKE THE MOST OF SEASONAL INGREDIENTS.

# GAZPACHO

ORIGINALLY FROM ANDALUSIA IN SPAIN, THIS CHILLED SOUP IS A REFRESHING CHOICE FOR A HOT SUMMER DAY.

—

**SERVES 6**

**PREP TIME** 20 minutes, plus
   chilling

—

875 g (1¾ lb) tomatoes,
   skinned and roughly
   chopped

½ cucumber, roughly
   chopped

2 red peppers, deseeded
   and roughly chopped

1 stick celery, chopped

2 garlic cloves, chopped

½ red chilli, deseeded and
   sliced

small handful of coriander
   or flat leaf parsley, plus
   extra to garnish

2 tablespoons white wine
   vinegar

2 tablespoons sun-dried
   tomato paste

4 tablespoons olive oil

salt

**TO SERVE**

ice cubes

hard-boiled egg, finely
   chopped

a little cucumber, pepper
   and onion, finely chopped

**1** Mix together the vegetables, garlic, chilli and coriander in a large bowl.

**2** Add the vinegar, tomato paste, oil and a little salt. Process in batches in a food processor or blender until smooth, scraping the mixture down from the sides of the bowl if necessary.

**3** Collect the blended mixtures together in a clean bowl and check the seasoning, adding a little more salt if needed. Chill for up to 24 hours before serving.

**4** To serve, ladle the gazpacho into bowls, scatter with ice cubes and garnish with chopped parsley or coriander and a little chopped hard-boiled egg, cucumber, pepper and onion, if wished.

# MINT, SPINACH & BUTTERMILK SOUP

THE BUTTERMILK IN THIS SOUP HAS TART FLAVOUR AND IS HIGH IN BONE-BUILDING CALCIUM.

—

**SERVES 4**

**PREP TIME** 10 minutes

—

250 g (8 oz) frozen spinach, defrosted

1 garlic clove, crushed

1 teaspoon mild curry powder

½ teaspoon peeled and finely grated fresh root ginger

500 ml (17 fl oz) buttermilk

6 tablespoons finely chopped mint leaves, plus extra to garnish

350 ml (12 fl oz) iced water

8 ice cubes

salt and pepper

—

**1** Place the spinach in a colander and squeeze out the excess water. Chop the spinach very finely.

**2** Transfer to a food processor with the garlic, curry powder, ginger and buttermilk. Season well and stir in the chopped mint. Add the measured water and process the mixture until smooth.

**3** Ladle the soup into chilled bowls, drop 2 ice cubes into each bowl and garnish with a few extra mint leaves. Serve immediately.

# CRUNCHY THAI-STYLE SALAD

THE RED CABBAGE IN THIS COLOURFUL SALAD HAS A PEPPERY FLAVOUR AND WEALTH OF VITAMINS AND MINERALS, INCLUDING COPPER AND MANGANESE.

—

**SERVES 2**

**PREP TIME** 10 minutes

—

2 carrots

1 courgette

½ small red cabbage, finely shredded

1 yellow pepper, cored, deseeded and thinly sliced

4 spring onions, finely sliced

2 tablespoons chopped fresh coriander

150 g (5 oz) rice noodles

### DRESSING

1 red chilli, deseeded and chopped

4 tablespoons Thai fish sauce

grated rind and juice of 1 lime

2 tablespoons caster sugar

—

**1** Use a potato peeler to shred the carrots and courgette into fine slices. Toss together the sliced vegetables with the cabbage, pepper, spring onions and coriander.

**2** Cook the noodles in boiling water according to the instructions on the packet, drain and leave to cool. Make the dressing by whisking together the chilli, Thai fish sauce, lime rind and juice and sugar in a small bowl. Mix the noodles with the vegetables. Toss the dressing through the salad and serve.

# CHICORY, MACKEREL & ORANGE SALAD

ALSO CALLED ENDIVE, CHICORY CAN BE ENJOYED COOKED OR RAW, AS IN THIS CITRUSSY SALAD.

—

**SERVES 2**

**PREP TIME** 10 minutes

—

2 heads of chicory

2 mackerel fillets, flaked

2 oranges, segmented

handful of watercress

**DRESSING**

juice of 1 orange

1 tablespoon olive oil

1 teaspoon wholegrain mustard

1 teaspoon clear honey

—

**1** Separate the chicory into individual leaves and mix them in a large bowl with the mackerel, orange segments and watercress.

**2** To make the dressing, whisk together the orange juice, oil, mustard and honey.

**3** Drizzle the dressing over the salad and serve with crusty bread.

# SMOKED SALMON SUSHI SALAD

NORI IS AN EDIBLE JAPANESE SEAWEED THAT IS SHREDDED AND DRIED AND IS AVAILABLE READY-TOASTED AND READY TO USE.

—

**SERVES 4**

**PREP TIME** 15 minutes

**COOKING TIME** 20 minutes

—

250 g (8 oz) sushi rice, well rinsed and very well drained

500 ml (17 fl oz) water

7 tablespoons rice vinegar

2 tablespoons caster sugar, plus an extra pinch

2 tablespoons sesame seeds

3 tablespoons soy sauce

2 teaspoons finely grated fresh root ginger

1 avocado, stoned, peeled and sliced

200 g (7 oz) smoked salmon slices

2 spring onions, sliced

2 tablespoons toasted, thinly sliced nori sheets, to garnish

salt

—

**1** Place the rice in a saucepan, pour over the measured water and season with salt. Bring to the boil, then cook for 10–12 minutes, until most of the water has boiled away and small craters appear in the rice. Cover with a tight-fitting lid and leave to steam off the heat for 5 minutes. Meanwhile, mix together 4 tablespoons of the vinegar and the 2 tablespoons sugar, until the sugar has dissolved.

**2** Tip the rice on to a baking sheet. Pour over the vinegar mixture and use a spatula to stir through in a slicing motion until the rice looks glossy. Cover with damp kitchen paper and leave to cool a little.

**3** Cook the sesame seeds in a small, dry frying pan over a low heat, until lightly browned.

**4** Mix together the remaining vinegar, soy sauce, ginger and the pinch of sugar. Spoon the rice into bowls. Arrange the avocado, smoked salmon and spring onions on top. Drizzle over the dressing. Cut the toasted nori into thin strips and scatter over with the sesame seeds.

# CORN, TOMATO & BLACK BEAN SALAD

ADDING A CREAMY CONTRAST TO THIS TEX-MEX SALAD, NUTRIENT-DENSE AVOCADO CONTAINS NEARLY 20 MINERALS AND VITAMINS.

—

—

**SERVES 4**

**PREP TIME** 10 minutes

**COOKING TIME** 10 minutes

—

4 corn cobs, leaves and fibres removed

250 g (8 oz) cherry tomatoes, halved

400 g (13 oz) can black beans, drained and rinsed

1 red onion, finely diced

1 avocado, peeled, stoned and diced

small bunch of coriander, roughly chopped

**DRESSING**

juice of 1 lime

2 tablespoons rapeseed oil

2—3 drops Tabasco sauce

**1** Cook the corn cobs in boiling water for 7–10 minutes. Cool briefly under running cold water then scrape off the kernels with a knife. Put the kernels in a large bowl with the tomatoes, black beans, onion and avocado and mix with the coriander.

**2** Make the dressing by mixing together the lime juice, oil and Tabasco.

**3** Drizzle the dressing over the salad, stir carefully to combine and serve immediately.

# HOT & SOUR CHICKEN SALAD

TOM YUM PASTE HAS A HOT AND SOUR FLAVOUR AND IS MADE UP OF A VARIETY OF INGREDIENTS, INCLUDING SHRIMP, GARLIC, LEMONGRASS AND CHILLI.

—

—

**SERVES 4**

**PREP TIME** 10 minutes

—

250 g (8 oz) ready-cooked chicken, roughly chopped

150 g (5 oz) salad leaves

125 g (4 oz) button mushrooms, thinly sliced

1 red chilli, deseeded and finely chopped

1 small bunch of fresh coriander, leaves stripped and chopped

1 tablespoon tom yum paste or Thai red curry paste

4 tablespoons vegetable oil

2 tablespoons lime juice

2 tablespoons roughly chopped roasted salted cashew nuts (optional)

**1** Toss the chicken in a large bowl with the salad leaves, mushrooms, chopped chilli and coriander, then divide between 4 plates.

**2** Place the tom yum paste, vegetable oil and lime juice in a jar with a tight-fitting lid, then shake until thoroughly combined. Drizzle over the salad, scatter over the cashew nuts, if using, and serve immediately.

# WATERMELON, FENNEL & FETA SALAD

JUICY AND FULL OF VITAMIN C, WATERMELON COMBINES BRILLIANTLY WITH SALTY FETA IN THIS UNUSUAL SALAD.

—

—

**SERVES 4**

**PREP TIME** 10 minutes

**COOKING TIME** 2 minutes

—

350 g (11½ oz) fresh or frozen shelled broad beans

1 large fennel bulb

250 g (8 oz) watermelon flesh, diced

125 g (4 oz) feta cheese, crumbled

salt and pepper

### DRESSING

3 tablespoons extra-virgin olive oil

1 tablespoon lemon juice

1 teaspoon clear honey

1 teaspoon pomegranate syrup

**1** Cook the beans in a large saucepan of lightly salted boiling water for 2 minutes. Drain and immediately refresh under cold water. Pat dry with kitchen paper, then peel off and discard the tough outer skins. Put the beans in a bowl.

**2** Trim the fennel bulb. Cut in half, then crossways into wafer-thin slices. Add to the beans with the watermelon and feta.

**3** Whisk all the dressing ingredients together in a small bowl and season with salt and pepper. Pour over the salad, toss well and serve.

# COLD ASIAN SUMMER SOBA NOODLE SALAD

MIRIN, WHICH FEATURES IN THIS JAPANESE-INSPIRED RECIPE, IS A SWEET RICE WINE THAT IS CONSIDERED ESSENTIAL TO JAPANESE CUISINE.

—

**SERVES 4**

**PREP TIME** 10 minutes

—

625 g (1¼ lb) cooked soba noodles

2 carrots, finely julienned

6 spring onions, finely shredded

1 red pepper, finely sliced

4 tablespoons dark soy sauce

3 tablespoons sesame oil

1 tablespoon mirin

1 tablespoon caster sugar

½ teaspoon chilli oil

—

**1** Place the soba noodles in a wide bowl with the carrots, spring onions and pepper.

**2** In a separate bowl, mix together the soy sauce, sesame oil, mirin, sugar and chilli oil, then pour over the noodle mixture.

**3** Toss to mix well and serve chilled or at room temperature.

# FATTOUSH

**FATTOUSH IS A CLASSIC MIDDLE EASTERN SALAD THAT MAKES A GREAT LIGHT SUMMER MEAL.**

—

**SERVES 4-6**

**PREP TIME** 15 minutes

**COOKING TIME** 5 minutes

—

5 ripe tomatoes

1 cucumber

1 green pepper

1 red pepper

½ red onion

4 flat breads

2 tablespoons olive oil

salt and pepper

DRESSING

1 garlic clove, crushed

4 tablespoons lemon juice

3 tablespoons olive oil

2 tablespoons chopped
   parsley

2 tablespoons chopped
   mint

—

**1** Cut the tomatoes, cucumber, green and red peppers and onion into 1 cm (½ inch) pieces and put them in a non-metallic bowl.

**2** Cut the flat breads into 1 cm (½ inch) squares. Heat the oil in a frying pan and fry the bread in batches. Drain on kitchen paper and allow to cool.

**3** Make the dressing by whisking together the garlic, lemon juice, oil, parsley and mint.

**4** Pour the dressing over the vegetables, toss carefully and season to taste with salt and pepper. Garnish with the croutons and serve immediately.

# A BOWL FOR THE SOUL

WHEN YOU'VE HAD A TOUGH DAY, THE WEATHER IS GREY OR YOU SIMPLY NEED A CHEERING TREAT, CHOOSE A COMFORTING BOWL OF DELICIOUS GOODNESS TO FEED BODY AND SOUL FROM THIS CHAPTER.

# ORIENTAL RICE SOUP WITH EGG & GREENS

NAMED AFTER THE FRAGRANT JASMINE FLOWER, JASMINE IS A LONG-GRAIN RICE WITH A SUBTLE AROMA AND SOFT, STICKY TEXTURE.

—

—

**SERVES 4**

**PREP TIME** 15 minutes

**COOKING TIME** 20 minutes

—

4 spring onions

100 g (3½ oz) pak choi, roughly chopped

2 tablespoons vegetable oil

2.5 cm (1 in) piece root ginger, finely grated

2 garlic cloves, finely chopped

200 g (7 oz) jasmine rice

100 ml (3½ oz) rice wine

2 tablespoons soy sauce

1 teaspoons rice wine vinegar

1 litre (1¾ pints) hot vegetable stock (see page 125 for homemade)

4 eggs

1 tablespoon chilli oil, for drizzling

**1** Finely slice the spring onions, keeping the white and green parts separate. Combine the green bits with the pak choi in a bowl and set aside.

**2** Heat the oil gently in a saucepan. When hot, add the onion whites, ginger and garlic and stir-fry for 2–3 minutes.

**3** Add the rice, stir, then add the rice wine and bubble for a minute or so.

**4** Add the soy sauce, vinegar and stock and simmer, stirring occasionally, for 10–12 minutes. Then stir in the reserved spring onions and pak choi and cook for a further 2–3 minutes. Meanwhile, poach the eggs in two batches.

**5** To serve, ladle the soup into bowls and top each one with a poached egg and drizzle over the chilli oil.

# SPICED TOMATO & CHORIZO SOUP

CHORIZO – A SPANISH PORK SAUSAGE SEASONED WITH CHILLI AND PAPRIKA – ADDS A HINT OF HEAT TO EVERYONE'S FAVOURITE, TOMATO SOUP.

—

**SERVES 4**

**PREP TIME** 10 minutes

**COOKING TIME** 15 minutes

—

3 tablespoons olive oil

1 red onion, chopped

2 garlic cloves, chopped

1 teaspoon hot smoked paprika

2 x 400 g (13 oz) cans butter beans, chopped

100 g (3½ oz) sun-dried tomatoes, drained

500 g (1 lb) passata

900 ml (1½ pints) vegetable stock (see page 125 for homemade)

150 g (5 oz) chorizo, diced

salt and pepper

chopped parsley, to garnish

crusty bread, to serve

—

**1** Heat 2 tablespoons of the oil in a large saucepan or flameproof casserole dish and cook the onion and garlic over a medium heat for 4–5 minutes, until slightly softened.

**2** Add the paprika and butter beans and stir for 1 minute before adding the sun-dried tomatoes, passata and stock. Bring to the boil, then simmer for about 10 minutes, until thickened slightly.

**4** Meanwhile, heat the remaining oil in a small frying pan and cook the chorizo for 2–3 minutes, stirring frequently, until golden. Drain on kitchen paper and set aside.

**4** Blend the soup to the desired consistency, then season to taste and ladle into bowls. Top with the chorizo and parsley and serve immediately with plenty of crusty bread.

# LENTIL & PEA SOUP

EXCLUSIVELY CULTIVATED IN THE REGION OF LE PUY IN CENTRAL FRANCE, PUY LENTILS ARE A SUPERB SOURCE OF VEGGIE PROTEIN.

**SERVES 4**

**PREP TIME** 10 minutes

**COOKING TIME** 2 hours

1 teaspoon olive oil

1 leek, finely sliced

1 garlic clove, crushed

400 g (13 oz) can Puy lentils, drained

2 tablespoons chopped mixed herbs, such as thyme and parsley

200 g (7 oz) frozen peas

2 tablespoons crème fraîche

1 tablespoon chopped mint

pepper

## VEGETABLE STOCK

1 tablespoon olive oil

1 onion, chopped

1 carrot, chopped

4 celery sticks, chopped

any vegetable trimmings, such as celery tops, onion skins and tomato skins

1 bouquet garni

1.3 litres (2¼ pints) water

salt and pepper

**1** To make the stock, heat the oil in a large saucepan, add the vegetables and fry for 2–3 minutes, then add the vegetable trimmings and bouquet garni and season well. Pour over the measured water, bring to the boil and simmer gently for 1½ hours, by which time the stock should have reduced to 900 ml (1½ pints). Drain over a bowl, discarding the vegetables and retaining the stock.

**2** Heat the oil in a medium saucepan, add the leek and garlic and fry over a gentle heat for 5–6 minutes until the leek is softened.

**3** Add the lentils, stock and herbs, bring to the boil and simmer for 10 minutes. Add the peas and continue to cook for 5 minutes.

**4** Transfer half the soup to a liquidizer or food processor and blend until smooth. Return to the pan, stir to combine with the unblended soup, then heat through and season with plenty of pepper.

**5** Stir together the crème fraîche and mint and serve on top of each bowl of soup.

# GREEK LAMB WITH TZATZIKI TOASTS

SHARE A STEAMING BOWL OF THIS SUCCULENT, SLOW-COOKED STEW WITH FRIENDS ON A WINTER NIGHT.

—

—

**SERVES 4**

**PREP TIME** 15 minutes

**COOKING TIME** 1½ hours

—

750 g (1½ lb) lamb chump chops

2 teaspoons dried oregano

3 garlic cloves, crushed

4 tablespoons olive oil

1 medium aubergine, about 300 g (10 oz), diced

2 red onions, sliced

200 ml (7 fl oz) white or red wine

400 g (13 oz) can chopped tomatoes

2 tablespoons clear honey

8 kalamata olives

8 thin slices French stick

200 g (7 oz) tzatziki

salt and pepper

**1** Cut the lamb into large pieces, discarding any excess fat. Mix the oregano with the garlic and a little seasoning and rub into the lamb.

**2** Heat half the oil in a large saucepan or sauté pan and fry the lamb in batches until browned. Drain to a plate.

**3** Add the aubergine to the pan with the onions and remaining oil and cook very gently, stirring frequently, for about 10 minutes, until softened and lightly browned. Return the meat to the pan with the wine, tomatoes, honey, kalamata olives and seasoning.

**4** Cover with a lid and cook on the lowest setting for about 1 hours or until the lamb is very tender. Lightly toast the bread and spoon the tzatziki on top.

**5** Check the stew for seasoning and turn into shallow bowls. Serve with the toasts on the side.

# LAMB MEATBALLS WITH FETA COUSCOUS

LAMB IS HIGH IN PROTEIN AS WELL AS PROVIDING YOU WITH ESSENTIAL IRON AND ZINC.

—

—

**SERVES 2**

**PREP TIME** 10 minutes

**COOKING TIME** 10 minutes

—

200 g (7 oz) lean minced lamb

1 garlic clove, crushed

½ teaspoon ground cumin

½ teaspoon ground coriander

2 tablespoons olive oil

salt and pepper

raita or tzatziki, to serve

## COUSCOUS

125 g (4 oz) couscous

1 tablespoon chopped parsley

1 tablespoon chopped mint leaves

50 g (2 oz) feta cheese, crumbled

75 g (3 oz) ready-cooked fresh beetroot, chopped

**1** Place the lamb in a bowl, add the garlic, cumin and coriander and season with salt and pepper. Mix well, then, using your hands, shape into 8 meatballs, pressing the mixture together firmly.

**2** Heat the oil in a frying pan, add the meatballs and fry over a medium heat for 8–10 minutes or until browned and cooked through.

**3** Meanwhile, place the couscous in a heatproof bowl and just cover with boiling water. Cover the bowl with clingfilm and leave to stand for 5 minutes. Fluff up the couscous with a fork, then season and stir in the herbs. Lightly stir through the feta and beetroot.

**4** Serve the meatballs with the couscous and generous spoonfuls of raita or tzatziki.

# SLOW-COOKED AROMATIC PORK CURRY

SHAPED LIKE AN EIGHT-POINTED STAR, STAR ANISE HAS AN ANISEED FLAVOUR THAT GOES PARTICULARLY WELL WITH PORK.

—

—

**SERVES 4**

**PREP TIME** 10 minutes

**COOKING TIME** 2½–3 hours

—

750 g (1½ lb) pork belly, trimmed and cubed

400 ml (14 fl oz) chicken stock

75 ml (3 fl oz) light soy sauce

finely grated rind and juice of 1 large orange

1 tablespoon peeled and finely shredded fresh root ginger

2 garlic cloves, sliced

1 dried red Kashmiri chilli

2 tablespoons medium curry powder

1 tablespoon hot chilli powder

1 tablespoon dark muscovado sugar

3 cinnamon sticks

3 cloves

10 black peppercorns

2–3 star anise

salt

**1** Place the pork in a large saucepan or casserole, cover with water and bring to the boil over a high heat. Cover, reduce the heat and simmer gently for 30 minutes. Drain and return the pork to the pan with the remaining ingredients. Season to taste.

**2** Add just enough water to cover the pork and bring to the boil over a high heat. Cover tightly, reduce the heat to low and cook very gently for 1½ hours, stirring occasionally.

**3** Remove the lid and simmer, uncovered, for 30 minutes, stirring occasionally, until the meat is meltingly tender. Serve with steamed Asian greens and rice.

# CHICKEN & BARLEY RISOTTO

THIS IS A HEALTHY TAKE ON RISOTTO, USING BARLEY, WHICH HAS A NUTTY TEXTURE AND PROVIDES A RANGE OF IMPORTANT VITAMINS AND MINERALS.

—

**SERVES 4**

**PREP TIME** 15 minutes

**COOKING TIME** about 1 hour 10 minutes

—

2 tablespoons olive oil

6 boneless, skinless chicken thighs, diced

1 onion, roughly chopped

2 garlic cloves, finely chopped

200 g (7 oz) chestnut mushrooms, sliced

250 g (8 oz) pearl barley

200 ml (7 fl oz) red wine

1.2 litres (2 pints) chicken stock

salt and pepper

parsley leaves, to garnish

Parmesan, if desired

—

**1** Heat the oil in a large frying pan over a medium-high heat, add the chicken and onion and fry for 5 minutes, stirring until lightly browned.

**2** Stir in the garlic and mushrooms and fry for 2 minutes, then mix in the pearl barley. Add the red wine, half the stock and season with plenty of salt and pepper, then bring to the boil, stirring continuously. Reduce the heat, cover and simmer for 1 hour, topping up with extra stock as needed, until the chicken is cooked through and the barley is soft.

**3** Spoon into bowls and garnish with the parsley and sprinkle with grated Parmesan. Serve with garlic bread and salad, if desired.

# QUICK COQ AU VIN

FOR WHEN YOU WANT A SPECIAL TREAT BUT DON'T HAVE A LOT OF TIME, THIS VERSION OF THE CLASSIC DISH IS IDEAL.

—

**SERVES 4**

**PREP TIME** 10 minutes

**COOKING TIME** 25 minutes

—

2 tablespoons olive oil

8 chicken drumsticks

8 streaky bacon rashers, roughly chopped

8 whole shallots

250g (8oz) chestnut mushrooms, halved

1 tablespoon plain flour

2 tablespoons thyme leaves

300ml (½ pint) red wine

450ml (¾ pint) chicken stock

sprigs of thyme, to garnish

mashed potatoes, to serve

**1** Heat the oil in a large, heavy based frying pan, add the drumsticks and bacon and cook over a high heat for 5 minutes. Add the shallots and mushrooms and cook for a further 5 minutes, turning the chicken and shallots, until golden all over. Add the flour and toss to coat, then add the thyme.

**2** Pour in the wine and stock and bring to the boil, stirring continually to distribute the flour evenly within the sauce. Reduce the heat and simmer, uncovered, for 15 minutes until the chicken is cooked through.

**3** Garnish the coq au vin with thyme, springs and serve ladled on to hot mashed potatoes in bowls.

# PUMPKIN & ROOT VEGETABLE STEW

PACKED WITH HEALTHY ROOT VEG, THIS STEW IS EVEN BETTER THE NEXT DAY. SERVE WITH CRUSTY BREAD OR GARLIC MASHED POTATOES FOR AN ADDED COMFORT FACTOR.

—

**SERVES 8–10**

**PREP TIME** 20 minutes

**COOKING TIME** 1½–2 hours

—

1 pumpkin, about 1.5 kg (3 lb)

4 tablespoons sunflower or olive oil

1 large onion, finely chopped

3–4 garlic cloves, crushed

1 small red chilli, deseeded and chopped

4 celery sticks, cut into 2.5 cm (1 inch) lengths

500 g (1 lb) carrots, cut into 2.5 cm (1 inch) pieces

250 g (8 oz) parsnips, cut into 2.5 cm (1 inch) pieces

2 x 400g (13 oz) cans plum tomatoes

3 tablespoons tomato purée

1–2 tablespoons hot paprika

250 ml (8 fl oz) vegetable stock (see page 125 for homemade)

1 bouquet garni

2 x 400 g (13 oz) cans red kidney beans, drained

salt and pepper

3–4 tablespoons finely chopped parsley, to garnish

—

**1** Slice the pumpkin in half across its widest part and discard the seeds and fibres. Cut the flesh into cubes, removing the skin. You should have about 1 kg (2 lb) pumpkin flesh.

**2** Heat the oil in a large saucepan and fry the onion, garlic and chilli until soft but not coloured. Add the pumpkin and celery and fry gently for 10 minutes. Stir in the carrots, parsnips, tomatoes, tomato purée, paprika, stock and bouquet garni. Bring to the boil, then reduce the heat, cover the pan and simmer for 1–1½ hours until the vegetables are almost tender.

**3** Add the beans and cook for 10 minutes. Season with salt and pepper and garnish with the parsley to serve.

# SPINACH DHAL WITH CHERRY TOMATOES

GARAM MASALA IS A WARMING AND AROMATIC BLEND OF SPICES – 'MASALA' MEANS SPICE – THAT IS USED IN MANY INDIAN DISHES.

—

**SERVES 4**

**PREP TIME** 10 minutes

**COOKING TIME** 30 minutes

—

300 g (10 oz) red split lentils

200 ml (7 oz) coconut milk

600 ml (1 pint) vegetable stock (see page 125 for homemade)

1 teaspoon ground cumin

1 teaspoon ground coriander

1 teaspoon turmeric

1 teaspoon ground ginger

300 g (10 oz) spinach, chopped

200 g (7 oz) cherry tomatoes

¼ teaspoon garam masala

25 g (1 oz) coriander (leaves and stalks), chopped

salt and pepper

naan bread or rice, to serve

TARKA

2 tablespoons sunflower oil

4 shallots, thinly sliced

3 garlic cloves, thinly sliced

1 teaspoon finely chopped ginger

¼ teaspoon chilli powder

2 teaspoons cumin seeds

1 teaspoon black mustard seeds

**1** Place the lentils in a sieve and rinse under cold running water until the water runs clear. Drain and transfer to a wide saucepan with the coconut milk, stock, cumin, coriander, turmeric and ginger. Bring the mixture to the boil, skimming off any scum as it rises to the surface, and then cover. Reduce the heat and simmer for 15–20 minutes, stirring occasionally to prevent the mixture from sticking to the base of the saucepan.

**2** Stir in the spinach and cherry tomatoes and cook for 6–8 minutes, or until the lentils are soft and tender, adding a little stock or water if the mixture seems too thick.

**3** Meanwhile, make the tarka. Heat the oil in a small frying pan and sauté the shallots, garlic, ginger, chilli powder, and cumin and mustard seeds, stirring often. Cook for 3–4 minutes until the shallots are lightly browned, and then scrape this mixture into the cooked lentils.

**4** Stir in the garam masala and chopped coriander into the lentil mixture, then check the seasoning. Serve with naan bread or rice.

# INDEX

# PICTURE ACKNOWLEDGEMENTS

**DREAMSTIME.COM** Arinahabich08 2, 9 cr; Annapustynnikova 96 bl; Annashepulova 9 br, 31 bl, 97 cr; Antoine Beyeler 97 cl; Baloncici 96 ar; Bhofack2 75 al; Bubutu 9 cl; Corinna Gissemann 31 cl; Danil Roudenko 31 br; Elxeneize 52 bl; Erica Schroeder 8 cr, 119 bl; Gkuna 7, 74 al; Haveseen 31 ar; Hdconnelly 8 br; Jasmina976 5; Jirkaejc 75 cr; Kondratova 53 al; 119 ar; Konstantin Kamenetskiy 96 al; Kuzelv 96 bc; Leerobin 30 cl; Long Ly Hoang 52 bc; Luke Wilcox 8 al; Izf 74 bc; Maksim Luhouski 8 bl; Marcin Jucha 52 ar; Marina Pissarova 119 cr; Miloszg 118 b; Mustipan 30 al; Mythja 9 bl; 53 cr, 97 al; Pyroshot 30 cr, 96 cr; Raluca Tudor 52 cr; Seqoya 8 ac, 30 br; Sihasakprachum 53 ar; stockcreations 53 br; Studiobarcelona 30 ac; Tomert 75 br, 119 al; Viktor Pravdica 9 ar; Yajai Kaewkam 74 ar; Yulia Grigoryeva 74 b; Zkruger 53 cl.

**OCTOPUS PUBLISHING GROUP** Craig Robertson 98; David Munns 13, 43, 132; Ian Wallace 18, 35, 65, 84, 113; Lis Parsons 25, 32, 39, 44, 51, 62, 76, 79, 87, 109, 117, 127, 128, 135, 136; Stephen Conroy 21, 47, 48, 57, 58, 61, 69, 70, 95, 102, 105; Will Heap 22, 36, 40, 91, 92, 101, 114, 120, 123, 131, 139; William Reavell 80, 110; William Shaw 10, 14, 17, 26, 29, 54, 66, 73, 83, 88, 106, 124.

**SHUTTERSTOCK** Annette Shaff 119 br; Anton Watman 97 ar; casanisa 118 al; dp Photography 52 al; Dustin Dennis 75 ar; Gertan 30 bl; Imaake 118 ar; Martchan 118 cr; meaofoto 97 br; Sebastiana 74 cr; stockcreations 119 cl; Yulia Grigoryeva 75 cl.